Watch me grow

Panda

LONDON, NEW YORK,
MELBOURNE, MUNICH, and DELHI

Written and edited by Fleur Star
and Lorrie Mack
Designed by Bookwork and Gemma Fletcher
Jacket editor Mariza O'Keeffe
Production editor Sean Daly

Publishing manager Susan Leonard
Art director Rachael Foster

Consultant Sarah M. Bexell, PhD
Director of Conservation Education
at the Chengdu Research Base
of Giant Panda Breeding
Chengdu photographs Zhang Zhihe, PhD
Director of the Chengdu Research Base
of Giant Panda Breeding
www.panda.org.cn

First published in the United States in 2008 by
DK Publishing
375 Hudson Street, New York, New York, 10014

Copyright © 2008 Dorling Kindersley Limited

08 09 10 11 12 10 9 8 7 6 5 4 3
WD162 – 12/07

A catalog record for this book
is available from the Library of Congress.

Hardback edition ISBN 978-0-7566-3432-2
Paperback edition ISBN 978-0-7566-3888-7

Color reproduction by MDP, UK
Printed and bound in China by
South China Printing Co. Ltd.

Discover more at
www.dk.com

Contents

🐼 I'm a giant panda

I'm a bear that lives in China. I have thick black and white fur. I spend half my day eating bamboo. The rest of the time I like to sleep and play—just like you!

Super senses

Pandas have a keen sense of smell. Their hearing is excellent, too, which is why they're hard to find—when they hear people coming, they leave!

Pandas have thick, oily fur to keep out the cold and wet weather.

Now turn the page and see how I grow...

Furry paws help pandas to walk on slippery snow and steep rocks.

Their teeth are strong enough to bite through thick bamboo stems.

5

🐼 This is my home

Pandas live in China, in the mountains where bamboo grows. In the wild, they don't live anywhere else in the world. Bamboo is the panda's favorite food.

A different home

Jing Jing was born at Chengdu Panda Base, in China. Her mother and father live there, too. She has keepers to help look after her.

Time for a rest

Pandas find resting places in bamboo groves or rock dens. Young pandas rest in trees.

Winter in the mountains can be very cold and snowy.

🐼 This is my mom

Jing Jing's mother is named Ya Ya. When she gave birth to Jing Jing, her cub was taken to be weighed and checked, but was soon given back to Mom to be looked after.

Bear facts

. . . .

🐼 Panda moms usually give birth to one or two cubs at a time.

🐼 Cubs stay with their mom for at least 18 months. Some stay longer.

🐼 It takes about five years for a female cub to become an adult, but up to seven years for a male.

Nothing beats a hug from Mom!

Early days

A newborn panda cub is tiny—about as long as a pencil! It's born with a bit of white fur.

At 15 days old, I haven't changed much. My skin is still mostly pink.

... But about five days later, you can see where my black fur will grow.

I get weighed as I grow. This way, my keepers can be sure Mom is looking after me and I'm eating well.

I'm two months old

Adult pandas live alone. The only time an adult lives with another panda is when a mom live with her cub. Panda dads don't get involved.

I can't walk yet, so I stay very close to Mom.

Sleepy head

Panda cubs sleep a lot of the time, just like human babies. Even full-grown pandas spend nearly half their days resting.

Mommy and me

Ya Ya, Jing Jing's mom, has other cubs who are older than Jing Jing, so Ya Ya knows all about how to be a mom.

🐼 Reaching new heights

I'm an expert at climbing trees! My arms and legs are short, but they are strong. It took a lot of practice, but now I can pull myself up and hang on. I grip the branches with my sharp claws.

A place to think
After all that climbing, it's good to stop and rest. Panda cubs spend a lot of time up in trees, where they're safe from predators

In the mating season, a female panda sometimes climbs a tree while males fight over her on the ground.

🐼 Time for dinner

Now I'm eight months old, I am starting to explor
solid food. My main food is bamboo, which I learn
to eat by copying Mom. Bamboo doesn't give me
much energy, so I need to eat a lot of it. I spend
most of my day eating and resting.

Bamboo facts

- Bamboo can grow up to 3 ft (1 m) a day. That's fast!
- Bamboo can grow in hot places, cold places, high places, and low places.
- There are hundreds of different species of bamboo in China.

Drinking water
In the wild, pandas often
live near rivers so they
have lots of water to drink.

Yum! Sweet, juicy bamboo!

Bamboo shoots
are the pandas'
favorite food.

15

Panda's playtime

Pandas love to play! In the wild, mums and cubs play together. This is how the cub learns. Adult pandas live and play alone.

Let's try the swing

I'm up here now

Play and learn

At the Chengdu Panda Base, Jing Jing has a bamboo climbing frame. The cubs at Chengdu are given these special playgrounds so they can practice climbing while they play.

Life at Chengdu

The Chengdu Research Base of Giant Panda Breeding in China works to save giant pandas. Today there are 47 pandas being looked after at the base.

Chengdu is in central China. The base is near a city, but was built to look like a panda's natural forest home.

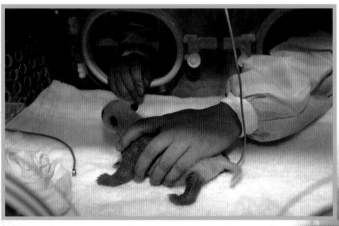

Looking after the pandas

Pandas in Chengdu have a whole team of staff to help care for them. Vets check their health from the moment they are born, and keepers feed and play with cubs as part of looking after them.

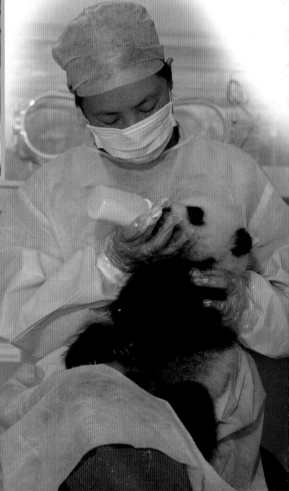

Enclosures

At Chengdu, a panda's enclosure is full of things a panda loves, such as climbing frames, a pool, and toys. Adult pandas live alone, but young pandas sometimes share.

Jing Jing

The star of this book, Jing Jing, was born at Chengdu in August 2005. She has been chosen as one of the mascots of the Beijing Olympics.

Jing Jing was just over two years old when this book was made. She shares her enclosure, and her keepers, with two other young pandas—but not her bamboo!

Breeding success

Giant pandas are an endangered species. There are fewer than 1,900 left in the world. Places like Chengdu help to conserve (or save) the species by helping their pandas breed.

These are some of the 12 pandas born in 2006.

Education

At Chengdu, visitors learn about pandas, and also about conservation— how to look after our planet and the animals we share it with.

Baby boom

Jing Jing is one of 45 pandas that have been born at Chengdu since the year 2000... so far!

A job for life

There are only about 240 captive pandas in the world. They are all part of a breeding program to help them have cubs. Being a mother will become Jing Jing's job, too!

The circle of life goes around and around

Now you know how I turned into a grown-up panda.

Glossary

Bamboo
A kind of giant grass with tough, hollow stems.

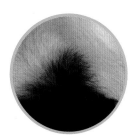

Fur
The thick, hairy coat that keeps an animal warm.

Claw
One of the short, sharp, curved nails on an animal's paw.

Keeper
Someone who looks after animals in a zoo or center.

Cub
A baby bear (or fox, or lion) in its first year.

Predator
An animal that kills and eats other animals.

Acknowledgments
The publisher would like to thank the following for their kind permission to reproduce their photographs: (Key: a=above; c=center; b=below; l=left; r=right; t=top)

Alamy Images: Steve Bloom Images 1, 6-7; LMR Group 22clb; Keren Su/ China Span 2-3; Andrew Woodley 5tr; Anna Yu 24crb. Ardea: M. Watson 22cb. Chengdu Research Base www.pandaphoto.com.cn: Zhang Zhihe 4crb, 6cr, 9c, 9ca, 10-11, 11ca, 11cr, 11tl, 12, 13cla, 13clb, 13r, 13tl, 14br, 14cl, 14-15, 16, 16tl, 17r, 17tl, 18br, 18cl, 18tr, 19br, 19clb, 19tl, 20-21, 21cr, 21tl, 22c, 22cr, 22tc, 22tr, 23, 24br, 24cla, 24clb, 24cra, 24tr. Corbis: Brooks Kraft 22crb; Phototex/epa 22cl; Reuters/Henry Romero 22tl. FLPA: Gerry Ellis/Minden Pictures 5cla, 6clb, 8-9, 9br, 9tr. OSF: Mike Powles 4cl. PA Photos: AP Photo/Color China Photo 20cl. Photoshot /NHPA: Gerard Lacz 4-5.

Jacket images: Front: Ardea: M. Watson tl. Getty Images: The Image Bank/Daniele Pellegrini tr; Minden Pictures/Gerry Ellis ftr. Back: Alamy Images: LMR Group clb. Ardea: M. Watson cb. Chengdu: c, cr, tc, tr. Corbis: Brooks Kraft crb; Phototex/epa cl; Reuters/Henry Romero tl. Getty Images: Minden Pictures/Cyril Ruoso/JH Editorial (b/g). Spine: Getty Images: The Image Bank/Daniele Pellegrini.

All other images © Dorling Kindersley For further information see: www.dkimages.com